MW01133876

Bee on a Swing

By Ruth Wolff, MS.Ed., Ph.D.

Illustrated by Simon Abbott

PETER PAUPER PRESS, INC.
Rye Brook, New York

Hank swings on a swing.

The strong sun makes Hank blink.

He doesn't see a bee
4 land on the swing.

Watch out, Hank!
Can you see the bee?

Zing goes the bee!
But will it sting?

Clink! Clank! Hank jumps off just in time.

The bee is alone.

See the flowers, bee!

A Big Mess!

By Ruth Wolff, MS.Ed., Ph.D.

Illustrated by Simon Abbott

PETER PAUPER PRESS, INC.
Rye Brook, New York

Molly Cat has a catnap
in the backyard.

Tom Tomcat sits on the backyard fence.

Into the yard slinks hungry
Bobtail Cat.

Bob spots a big trash can.

Clink! Clank!
Bob upsets the can.

Molly and Tom run to see
the big mess.

Meow! It's lunchtime for three happy cats!

8

LEVEL
C

A Picnic Basket

By Ruth Wolff, MS.Ed., Ph.D.

Illustrated by Simon Abbott

PETER PAUPER PRESS, INC.
Rye Brook, New York

Carlos and his twin sister Carla
get up with the sun.

It's the day of the big picnic!

Grandma packs a picnic basket
for the twins.

The twins unpack their basket
under a banyan tree.

Carlos and Carla each get a
pumpkin muffin and a cheese
sandwich for lunch.

Grandma didn't forget to pack
napkins and two cups for drinks.

7

What's this? Grandma put in a dessert!

At the Races

By Ruth Wolff, MS.Ed., Ph.D.

Illustrated by Simon Abbott

PETER PAUPER PRESS, INC.
Rye Brook, New York

Dogs love to race in the park.

Bats like to chase bugs
in the dark.

Cats will chase rats for fun.

And horses just love to run.

A tortoise will race a hare
on a dare.

FINISH

But why do people race for miles?

Just for fun, for some smiles,
and for a ribbon as a prize!

MY BEGINNING READERS

LEVEL
C

Campfire Cooks

By Ruth Wolff, MS.Ed., Ph.D.

Illustrated by Simon Abbott

PETER PAUPER PRESS, INC.
Rye Brook, New York

Sam Cook makes a pancake

2 on the campfire.

Sam makes a crabcake, too.

Inside the tent, Emmy Cook
frosts cupcakes.

4

She shakes up a milkshake, too.

Wait! Who is there?

Big Bear pokes his
nose in the tent.

Big Bear bakes a cheesecake. Yum! Yum!

MY BEGINNING READERS

LEVEL C

Costume Party

By Ruth Wolff, MS.Ed., Ph.D.

Illustrated by Simon Abbott

PETER PAUPER PRESS, INC.
Rye Brook, New York

Jess invites her friends to a party. She wants each one to wear a costume.

Luca will dress up as a ragdoll.

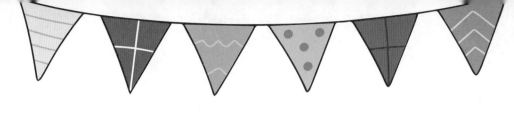

Ali can be a rock star.

Jayden makes a vampire costume.

5

Kayla wants to be an umpire.

6

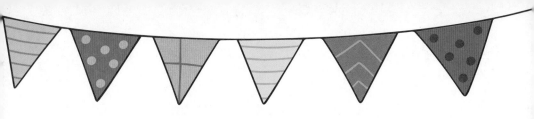

What will Jess be? Oh, no!
She cannot decide.

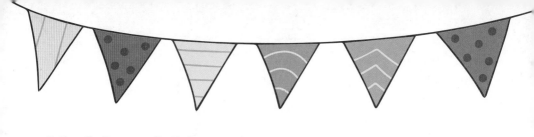

Hold on! Her costume will be
a big surprise.

A Lucky Rabbit

By Ruth Wolff, MS.Ed., Ph.D.

Illustrated by Simon Abbott

PETER PAUPER PRESS, INC.
Rye Brook, New York

A fluffy rabbit
hops onto a grassy yard.

It spies a carrot patch.

3

Hop! Hop!
Into the garden it goes.

"How lucky am I?"
thinks the rabbit.

But yikes! A large dog guards the garden.

The rabbit grabs a carrot and hops away.

"What a lucky rabbit am I!"
says the rabbit.

8

Maisy at the Spa

By Ruth Wolff, MS.Ed., Ph.D.

Illustrated by Simon Abbott

PETER PAUPER PRESS, INC.
Rye Brook, New York

Maisy goes to the King Charles Dog Spa.

She checks in
at the front desk.

3

It's time to get her nails cut.

A day at the spa is not complete without a haircut.

Maisy gets a bath, too.

How nice Maisy looks!

She cannot wait for another
day at the spa.

MY BEGINNING READERS

LEVEL
C

Danny Deer

By Ruth Wolff, MS.Ed., Ph.D.

Illustrated by Simon Abbott

PETER PAUPER PRESS, INC.
Rye Brook, New York

A peach hangs on a leafy green tree.

Danny Deer sees the peach.

"I want to eat that peach for lunch," thinks Danny.

**But Danny must leap
over a fence to get the peach.**

"Dear me," he says.
"Can I do it?"

6

What a leap! What a reach!

7

Yum! Yum! What a sweet peach!

MY BEGINNING READERS

LEVEL
C

Billy the Goat

By Ruth Wolff, MS.Ed., Ph.D.

Illustrated by Simon Abbott

PETER PAUPER PRESS, INC.
Rye Brook, New York

Billy is an old goat.

2

When he was a kid, Billy could run fast!

He was the star of the herd.

"We want Billy on our team," the other goats would say.

But now Billy
moans and groans
when he sees a hill.

6

"Can I climb this hill?" he asks himself.

7

Slow but sure, he makes it
to the top. Billy is still a star!

MY BEGINNING READERS

LEVEL C

A Snowplow

By Ruth Wolff, MS.Ed., Ph.D.

Illustrated by Simon Abbott

PETER PAUPER PRESS, INC.
Rye Brook, New York

Snowplow clears the snow
2 **from the roads.**

Snowplow is proud to clear
the snow.

3

"What a good job I do!" says
4 the plow.

But one day Snowplow makes a loud sound. "Screech!" "Ouch!"

5

Snowplow is stuck until the snow
melts in the spring.

"I cannot plow snow anymore," says the sad truck, frowning.

7

But Snowplow can go down South
to rest in the sun!

Night Flight

By Ruth Wolff, MS.Ed., Ph.D.

Illustrated by Simon Abbott

PETER PAUPER PRESS, INC.
Rye Brook, New York

What takes flight in the night?
A cat keeps watch. Its eyes
shine bright.

A pale moth opens its wings for a night flight.

A bat swoops by in the nighttime sky.

4

On silent wings, an owl glides through the dark.

Lightning bugs flash their lights at night.

6

Chirping crickets fly
to backyard lights.

7

And an airplane speeds
high in the sky as it goes to
far-off sights.

Callie the Camel

By Ruth Wolff, MS.Ed., Ph.D.

Illustrated by Simon Abbott

PETER PAUPER PRESS, INC.
Rye Brook, New York

Callie the Camel is going on a long trek in the desert.

2

Oh, no! Callie forgets
to pack her shoes.

Don't worry! Pads on her feet
4 protect her from the hot sand.

Oh, no! Callie cannot find her sunglasses.

Don't worry! Her long lashes
will keep the sun and sand
out of her eyes.

6

Wait! Callie lost her water jug.
And what about food?
Don't worry! Camels bring what
they need in their humps.

Callie doesn't need to pack
a thing!

8

A Fall Day

By Ruth Wolff, MS.Ed., Ph.D.

Illustrated by Simon Abbott

PETER PAUPER PRESS, INC.
Rye Brook, New York

Paul and Polly take their children, Austin and Audrey, to the park.

It is fall, and many leaves
are red and yellow.

3

Austin draws a sketch of a leaf.

Audrey wants to go on the seesaw.

5

Time to eat!
Paul and Polly unpack lunch.

What's inside? Crispy chicken, coleslaw, chips, and hot sauce for a dip. But where are the kids?

7

At the snack bar, eager
to get ice cream for dessert!

Frosting the Cake

By Ruth Wolff, MS.Ed., Ph.D.

Illustrated by Simon Abbott

PETER PAUPER PRESS, INC.
Rye Brook, New York

Megan and Matt are baking
a cake.

2

Megan is beating the eggs.

Helpful brother Matt is mixing
the batter.

4

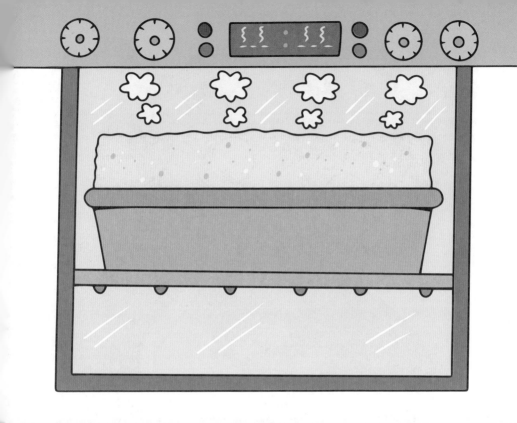

The cake is baking in the oven.
Smells good!

Time to make the frosting!

Playful pup Maisy wants to help, too.

Oh, no! Maisy adds a dog treat to the frosting when no one is looking!

MY BEGINNING READERS

LEVEL
C

Big Ben

By Ruth Wolff, MS.Ed., Ph.D.

Illustrated by Simon Abbott

PETER PAUPER PRESS, INC.
Rye Brook, New York

Big Ben is a big bell in a big clock tower.

Big Ben and its tower
have stood for more than
a hundred years.

Big Ben has rung as ships docked
on the river below.

It has rung as boats slipped under the bridges below.

Big Ben has tolled
as cars honked below.

6

Big Ben has tolled
as people shopped.

7

We hope Big Ben will never stop!

Ice Cream
Shakes

By Ruth Wolff, MS.Ed., Ph.D.

Illustrated by Simon Abbott

PETER PAUPER PRESS, INC.
Rye Brook, New York

Zack and Zoe Zebra were hungry.

"Let's grill hot dogs," said Zoe.

3

Zack grilled two hot dogs and two buns.

4

"Let's make ice cream shakes," said Zack.

Zoe got two tall glasses. First
Zoe went shake, shake, shake.

Then Zack went shake, shake, shake.

Two drinks fizzed and spilled.
Oh, no! Time for two zebras
to clean up the mess.

8

LEVEL
C

The Big Game

By Ruth Wolff, MS.Ed., Ph.D.

Illustrated by Simon Abbott

PETER PAUPER PRESS, INC.
Rye Brook, New York

It was the day of the big game!

Wildcat fans boarded a bus to get to the game.

Other fans drove there in cars.

More fans crowded on a train to get there.

5

Fans in the stands rooted for the Wildcats. "GO CATS, GO!"

The game ended with a big win for the team!

And the fans shouted, "Hooray!"

MY BEGINNING READERS

LEVEL C

Blue Bird

By Ruth Wolff, MS.Ed., Ph.D.

Illustrated by Simon Abbott

PETER PAUPER PRESS, INC.
Rye Brook, New York

One day a king received a gift— a bird named Blue.

Blue Bird sat on a swing in a cage of gold.

But Blue sang a sad song.

"Set me free, set me free," sang Blue.

"I want to fly away."

The king knew he had to set
Blue free. He opened the cage.

7

And away Blue flew!

The Mouse Cup

By Ruth Wolff, MS.Ed., Ph.D.

Illustrated by Simon Abbott

PETER PAUPER PRESS, INC.
Rye Brook, New York

It is time for the Mouse Cup soccer game!

It's the Field Mice against the House Mice.

Fred the Field Mouse uses his
long tail to smack the ball . . .

. . . but the ball just misses the net!

5

Harry the House Mouse jumps up and hits the ball with his head.

The House Mice score! The
sounds of squeaking, cheering
mice fill the air.

7

House Mouse Harry has won the Mouse Cup for his team!

MY BEGINNING READERS

LEVEL
C

Little Turtle

By Ruth Wolff, MS.Ed., Ph.D.

Illustrated by Simon Abbott

PETER PAUPER PRESS, INC.
Rye Brook, New York

Little Turtle swims alone
in a big tank.

He swims back and forth, back
and forth.

Little Turtle yawns.
He climbs onto a rock to rest.

But who is this on his rock?

Shy Little Turtle hides in his shell.

Don't be afraid, Little Turtle.
Meet your new friend, Tara Turtle!

Now two little turtles swim
back and forth, back and forth,
together.

MY BEGINNING READERS

LEVEL
C

A Magic Bubble

By Ruth Wolff, MS.Ed., Ph.D.

Illustrated by Simon Abbott

PETER PAUPER PRESS, INC.
Rye Brook, New York

Baby climbs on a chair
to reach the sink.

She fills a dish with soap
and water.

3

Baby dips a straw
into the soapy water . . .

. . . and blows a bubble.

She blows and blows, and the bubble grows and grows . . .

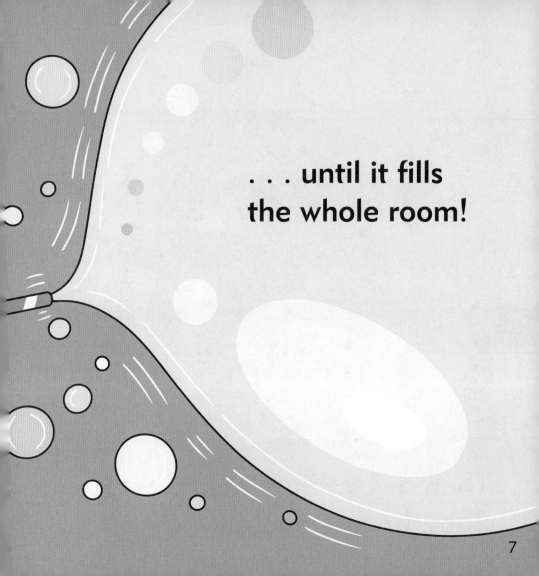

. . . until it fills
the whole room!

Then away floats the bubble,
Baby, house, and all!

8

MY BEGINNING READERS

LEVEL
C

Night on the Farm

By Ruth Wolff, MS.Ed., Ph.D.

Illustrated by Simon Abbott

PETER PAUPER PRESS, INC.
Rye Brook, New York

Papa puts the horse in the stable.

Papa hangs the saddle on the wall.

Mama ladles the soup.

4

Baby Jake sleeps in his cradle.

A candle glows in the dark.

A strong wind blows.

The candle goes out as snow
covers the farm.

8

LEVEL
C

Apple Betty

By Ruth Wolff, MS.Ed., Ph.D.

Illustrated by Simon Abbott

PETER PAUPER PRESS, INC.
Rye Brook, New York

Betty goes apple picking.

She fills a big basket with apples.

Betty makes apple pancakes
for lunch.

She tops the pancakes with thick maple syrup.

Betty bakes an apple pie
for dinner.

But the next day the basket
is empty!

Who took the apples from
Apple Betty?

Wiggly Bunny

By Ruth Wolff, MS.Ed., Ph.D.

Illustrated by Simon Abbott

PETER PAUPER PRESS, INC.
Rye Brook, New York

Uncle Rick gave Daisy a toy bunny.

The bunny could wiggle its ears
and nose.

Daisy could wiggle her ears and nose, too.

The bunny could wiggle its toes.

5

Daisy could wiggle her toes, too.

Daisy kept Wiggly Bunny in her toy box.

Daisy grew bigger and bigger,
but Wiggly Bunny stayed the
same, just for her.